REPLAY

PHILLIP KAVANAGH

CURRENT THEATRE SERIES

First published in 2016
by Currency Press Pty Ltd,
PO Box 2287, Strawberry Hills, NSW, 2012, Australia
enquiries@currency.com.au
www.currency.com.au

in association with Griffin Theatre Company

Copyright: *Replay* © Phillip Kavanagh, 2016.

COPYING FOR EDUCATIONAL PURPOSES
The Australian *Copyright Act 1968* (Act) allows a maximum of one chapter or 10% of this book, whichever is the greater, to be copied by any educational institution for its educational purposes provided that that educational institution (or the body that administers it) has given a remuneration notice to Copyright Agency Limited (CAL) under the Act.

For details of the CAL licence for educational institutions contact CAL, Level 15/233 Castlereagh Street, Sydney, NSW, 2000; tel: within Australia 1800 066 844 toll free; outside Australia 61 2 9394 7600; fax: 61 2 9394 7601; email: info@copyright.com.au

COPYING FOR OTHER PURPOSES
Except as permitted under the Act, for example a fair dealing for the purposes of study, research, criticism or review, no part of this book may be reproduced, stored in a retrieval system, or transmitted in any form or by any means without prior written permission. All enquiries should be made to the publisher at the address above.

Any performance or public reading of *Replay* is forbidden unless a licence has been received from the author or the author's agent. The purchase of this book in no way gives the purchaser the right to perform the play in public, whether by means of a staged production or a reading. All applications for public performance should be addressed to the author c/- Currency Press.

Cataloguing-in-publication data for this title is available from the National Library of Australia website: www.nla.gov.au

Typeset by Dean Nottle for Currency Press.
Cover image by Brett Boardman; front cover shows Alfie Gledhill.
Cover design by RE:.

Currency Press acknowledges the Traditional Owners of the Country on which we live and work. We pay our respects to all Aboriginal and Torres Strait Islander Elders, past and present.

Contents

REPLAY   1

Theatre Program at the end of the playtext

Replay was first produced by Griffin Theatre Company and Playwriting Australia at the Griffin Theatre, Sydney, on 2 April 2016, with the following cast:

MICHAEL / THERAPIST / ERIC	Jack Finsterer
JOHN / GEORGE	Alfie Gledhill
PETER / WILL	Anthony Gooley

Director, Lee Lewis
Designer, Tobhiyah Stone Feller
Lighting Designer, Benjamin Brockman
Composer and Sound Designer, Daryl Wallis
Stage Manager, Isabella Kerdijk

CHARACTERS

JOHN / WILL
PETER / GEORGE
MICHAEL / THERAPIST / ERIC

NOTES ON TEXT

A forward slash / marks the point of interruption for overlapping dialogue. At the end of a line it indicates that the next line cuts in immediately.

An interrupted line without punctuation at the end would have continued if not for the interruption.

A dash — denotes a terminated thought by the character speaking.

An ellipsis … indicates a trailing off in thought, or a hesitance to speak.

There should be no effort made to create a distinction between MICHAEL and the THERAPIST. When we first see the THERAPIST, we should initially mistake him for an adult MICHAEL. The characterisations of WILL, ERIC and GEORGE, however, should be distinctly different from the other roles played by those actors. The adoption of new characters should be readily apparent.

This play went to press before the end of rehearsals and may differ from the play as performed.

PROLOGUE

JOHN: I might, I might—I dunno—I might, I might—I dunno— / I might, I might

MICHAEL: Just jump.

JOHN: It's really high.

MICHAEL: You'll be fine.

PETER: No, you won't. This is crazy. Just climb down.

JOHN: I, I, I, /

PETER: Come on, I'll hold the ladder.

MICHAEL: He doesn't need the ladder. He's gonna jump.

PETER: I'll hold it steady. Guide your feet.

MICHAEL: Just aim for the centre, and boing … It's like flying.

PETER: You don't have to do this.

MICHAEL: He's not a pussy.

JOHN: I'm not a pussy, Peter.

PETER: I didn't say you / were.

JOHN: And I know what that means. And it doesn't mean cat.

PETER: It means cat too.

JOHN: Does it?

PETER: Yeah.

JOHN: Does it?

MICHAEL: Yeah.

JOHN: I need to apologise to Mary Martin.

MICHAEL: What did you do?

JOHN: I said some horrible things.

PETER: What?

JOHN: She said her pussy had fleas.

PETER and MICHAEL laugh together.

PETER: It'll be fine. Let's just get down and we can sort it out.

MICHAEL: Quickest way down is to jump.
PETER: Michael.
MICHAEL: He wants to. Don't you?
John?
JOHN: What if I land funny?
MICHAEL: Just aim centre and / you'll be fine.
PETER: You'll fall on the bricks and break your neck.
MICHAEL: Don't be a dick.
PETER: I don't want John to get hurt.
MICHAEL: You don't wanna lose ten dollars.
JOHN: What?
PETER: That was a separate thing.
JOHN: This is a bet?
PETER: Well … yeah, but that has / nothing to do with
MICHAEL: He didn't think you'd have the guts to jump.
JOHN: I've got more guts than you. I've got a whole bucketful of guts. And a yoyo.
PETER: The bet was a separate thing. I didn't want you to / get hurt.
JOHN: Stand back.
PETER: John.
MICHAEL: Good boy.
JOHN: Aim centre?
MICHAEL: You'll bounce straight up.
PETER: Don't.
MICHAEL: Hey, ten dollars, / ten dollars over here.
PETER: Shut up.
JOHN: I'm gonna—I'm gonna—I'm gonna—

JOHN jumps.

He lands poorly and bounces from the trampoline onto the bricks.

He screams out in pain.

MICHAEL: Fuck.
PETER: We are so dead.

PETER and MICHAEL rush to JOHN.

MICHAEL: Hey, hey. John. Johnny boy. / It's okay. Don't worry. You're fine. You're fine.
PETER: Oh, God. Is that blood? That's blood. We are so dead. Oh, God. Oh, God.
MICHAEL: You're not helping.
PETER: I'll get Mum.
MICHAEL: Wait.
What happened?
PETER: He jumped off the / roof.
MICHAEL: No. He was jumping on the trampoline. He slipped over and fell.
Didn't you?

JOHN is in too much pain to reply.

PETER: He jumped off the roof.
MICHAEL: Wanna bet?

Beat.

PETER: He was on the trampoline.
MICHAEL: Yep, yep. And then … you kicked a ball into him.
PETER: You kicked a ball into him.
MICHAEL: Okay. I kicked it.
But I was kicking it to you.
PETER: Fine.
MICHAEL: John?
JOHN: I was on the trampoline.
The ball hit my face.
I slipped. I fell.
MICHAEL: Good boy.
JOHN: You're always kicking balls at me.
MICHAEL: This was an accident.
JOHN: I'm always having accidents.

MICHAEL: You'll be fine. You're fine.
Get Mum.

SCENE ONE

JOHN: Thank you. For everything you said.
PETER: Don't even. Meant every word.
JOHN: That judge can be a stony-faced … statue, you know?
And when you were up there talking, saying what you said, she actually smiled.
I wasn't even sure she had teeth.
PETER: Happy to help.

Pause.

How is it living with Mum again? Murdered her yet?
JOHN: It's fine.
PETER: I couldn't imagine.
JOHN: Mum's alright.
She's away anyway.
PETER: Another camping trip?
JOHN: Yeah.
PETER: How are the … talks going?
JOHN: Going great. Really great.
PETER: Many bookings this week?
JOHN: Well, no, none this week. But next week I have two.
PETER: I suppose you might pick up some last minute.
JOHN: Two bookings in two weeks is good.
PETER: Is it?
JOHN: One of the teachers came up to me the other day and said, get this, 'That blew me away'. Me.
PETER: Wow.
JOHN: You should see the looks on their faces. These kids. I'll be standing there, just some guy, some guy who's been brought in to speak to them. 'Who's this guy?' they say.

PETER:	Do they?
JOHN:	No, their faces. That's what their faces say.
PETER:	Right. / Sorry.
JOHN:	Yeah, they don't actually say anything. Well, the older kids at the back do—they talk amongst themselves—just loud enough for me to know what they think of me— 'Who's this wanker?', you know, that sort of stuff—but when I start talking—the whispering stops, and the kids at the back … Pin drop.
PETER:	Really?
JOHN:	Tink tink. I open with the line, it's great, I say, 'I'm so sad'.
PETER:	And that stops them talking?
JOHN:	Oh yeah. Some grown-up standing there talking about his feelings? Oh yeah. And then I start to tell them / about God
PETER:	Are you?
JOHN:	What?
PETER:	Sad?
JOHN:	No, that's just … the opening line.
PETER:	Oh.
JOHN:	So … I say, 'I'm so sad', and they go silent, and then I start to tell them about God, about the relationship they can have with him … and their faces … jaw to the floor.
PETER:	But they're religious schools, aren't they?
JOHN:	Yeah.
PETER:	So, surely this isn't new to them. This … relationship with God.
JOHN:	Oh, sure, sure, but you're missing the best bit. They do have an understanding, that isn't new to them, no, but the best bit— I've introduced … a puppet.
PETER:	A puppet?

JOHN: Of Jesus.
Don't worry, don't worry, it's not offensive. I checked with a priest. He really likes my act. And, okay, it's unorthodox, but I get the puppet, and I hold him like, like this, and he goes between them and me, and I start talking to him, and he nods or shakes his head, and okay, it's, you know, I've established the convention. He'll respond but he won't speak. And then I ask, 'Does anyone have any questions for Jesus?' Only I don't call them questions. Do you want to know what I call them? Prayers.

PETER: Of course.

JOHN: They ask him their questions, their prayers, they pray to him, and for the first time, he talks back. And in that moment—as Jesus speaks directly to them—you should see their faces.

PETER: That sounds really rewarding.

JOHN: It is, yeah, it is.
I just wish … I wish I could see that look on more faces. You know? If I had more … more … resources, I could really … make it happen.
Do you know what I'm saying?

Pause.

PETER: Yeah. I do.

JOHN: If I can get this together, make this work, I really think it'll help. I might have a real shot with Jessie. Fifty-fifty.

PETER: Good odds.

JOHN: Joint custody.

PETER: Right. Sorry.

JOHN: Jessie's been practising her flower girl walk.

PETER: Has she?

JOHN: It's more of a dance than a walk. She sort of …

He tries to illustrate the movements of her dance/walk.

I can't do it. Don't have Jessie's sense of rhythm.

> The other day—as a joke—I said she should use the flowers in Mummy's garden to practise with.
> I didn't think she'd actually do it.
> Rebecca drove round just to yell at me.
> Fucking manipulative—Jessie sitting there in the back seat.
> Watching.
> Petals dropping from the car window.

Pause.

> I love this sofa. Where did you get it?

PETER: Freedom.

JOHN: Freedom? Freedom Furniture?

PETER: Yeah, Freedom Furniture.

JOHN: I went there once. Wanted a new sofa, walked out with a desk lamp.

PETER: You should write these things down.

JOHN: Should I?

PETER: So you don't forget.

JOHN: Am I forgetful?

PETER: You always forget things.

JOHN: Do I? I can't remember.

PETER: Well, there you go.

JOHN: What have I forgotten, Peter?

PETER: You forgot what you wanted from Freedom.

JOHN: Did I?

PETER: Did you want the desk lamp?

JOHN: No.
It's a really nice sofa.

PETER: Thank you.

Silence.

> John—
> I'd like to invest in your business.

JOHN: Peter, you don't have to / do that.

PETER: No, no.
JOHN: I know the wedding's costing you a lot.
PETER: Don't. I insist. This is head and shoulders better than the—what was it?—the llama farm?
JOHN: Yeah.
PETER: So don't mention it.
And, hey, it's tax deductable, right?
JOHN: No.
PETER: Well … It's an investment for me as much as you. I think there's a real future in … it.
JOHN: Thank you. I really— Thank you.

Silence.

PETER: Do you want a beer?
JOHN: Yeah, sure.

PETER *exits, leaving* JOHN *alone.*

Time passes.

JOHN *sits. Broken.*

He pulls out his phone. Makes a call.

Hi.
I know, I know we said that, but I just wanted to say hello to—
I know, and I'm not asking to see her, I just want—
It's not that much to—
Oh, you know what? Fuck you.
I'm sorry. I'm sorry I said that. I just—
I just wanna hear her voice. Can I just hear her voice?

Silence.

Hello.
Hello, honey. How, how have you been? Have you been good?

PETER *re-enters, unseen by* JOHN.

You give the babysitter a hard time today?

Good. Remember she has to earn her money, so you make her work for it.
Don't listen to her. It grows back.
I wish I'd been there.
Oh. Okay.
I love you.
Thanks, Bek, I really …
Yep. I won't. Sorry. 'Bye.

He hangs up.

Silence.

PETER: Here you go.

JOHN *rebuilds himself in an instant.*

JOHN: Thanks. Uh, cheers.
PETER: Yep. Cheers.
Shit, I never sent you the invite.
JOHN: What?

PETER *busies himself with his phone.*

PETER: Steve made them for Friday. It's great. There's this animated— No, no, won't spoil it. Sending. Sending. Sent.
JOHN: Received.
PETER: Open it, open it.
JOHN: 'Let's go stag … together'?
PETER: You know ad guys. All about the tagline. He workshopped that for days.
JOHN: Is that a deer?
PETER: A stag.
JOHN: Oh, I see, I see.
Oh, there are two of them.
PETER: Yeah, it's a play on words.
JOHN: I get it now, I get it.
He should've kept workshopping.
PETER: Got anything better?

JOHN: 'The buck starts here'?
PETER: I should've made you the best man.

Pause.

JOHN: Yeah.

SCENE TWO

THERAPIST: You don't know that.
JOHN: Steve will find a way.
THERAPIST: It could be fine.
JOHN: There'll be strippers peeling off designer lingerie we can buy from a stall up the back.
We'll be able to help ourselves to any drink we want, so long as it's this great new vodka that's just been launched.
The DJ will be flogging his album and the food will be served on oversized business cards.
THERAPIST: Advertising …
JOHN: The caterers, obviously.
THERAPIST: Right. Obviously.
JOHN: At least it's not themed.
THERAPIST: I dunno. That could be fun. Getting drunk surrounded by superheroes and Disney villains.
JOHN: What theme parties do you go to?
THERAPIST: Children's birthdays, mostly.
JOHN: Oh, right.
Steve's alright, I guess.
THERAPIST: And Peter?
JOHN: What do you mean?
THERAPIST: Sorry. I might be completely off base.
It just seemed like there was some tension there.
How is your relationship?
JOHN: With Peter?
THERAPIST: Yeah.

JOHN: It's fine.
We're good.
He's actually—he's helping me out. With the talks.
And he's been really supportive. With everything.
THERAPIST: How are the talks going?
JOHN: He's been great.
THERAPIST: I'm glad to hear it.
JOHN: Do you have brothers?
THERAPIST: No, I don't.
JOHN: Sisters?
THERAPIST: Yes. I have two.

Silence.

Do you want to talk about it?
JOHN: Not really.
THERAPIST: It's up to you.
We don't have to.
But we can.
JOHN: I'm just, I just don't know if I / want to
THERAPIST: That's fine.

Pause.

Michael, wasn't it?
JOHN: Sorry, I'm just not sure if I / want to
THERAPIST: Sure.
JOHN: It's just that / I
THERAPIST: You don't have to.

Pause.

JOHN: Yeah.
Yes.
Michael. His name.
Michael.

Pause.

THERAPIST: What happened?

JOHN: I, um…
I … was young. I was really young. Still old enough to— I still remember him. Well.
It was an accident.

Silence.

THERAPIST: Do you need to / take a

JOHN: No, I'm—
We went hiking. We used to go all the time. And, um, Peter and Michael ran off without me. Always did. I could never keep up. But this one time—this one day—Michael was—he was running too fast.
And he stumbled. At the top of the trail. And he fell off the cliff.
He, um, the impact—
His neck. Snapped.
It was instant.

THERAPIST: How old were you?

JOHN: I'm fine. I was a kid. I, you know, I remember him, he was my big brother, but I'm fine.
It affected Peter pretty bad.
He was there.
Saw it happen.
He wasn't … He wasn't in a good place for a long time.
I was fine.

THERAPIST: You don't have to be. If you're not. You don't have to be fine.

Pause.

JOHN: I used to—after—for a bit—I used to see this image. As in, always, always see this image. I'd blink and it would flash.

THERAPIST: What was it?

JOHN: The moment I finally caught up to them.
At the top.
Peter on his knees. Crying.
And Michael's gone.

THERAPIST: Do you still see it?
JOHN: Sometimes, I ... Yeah.
Yeah, I do.
THERAPIST: Can we try something?
JOHN: What?
THERAPIST: Just an exercise.
Can I get you to close your eyes?
JOHN: Um ... Yeah.
THERAPIST: Now, I want you to think back to that day. But before. Before you reach the top of the cliff. Well before that image.
What do you see?
JOHN: Um ... Leaves. And branches, obviously.
Trees.
Even more obvious.
THERAPIST: And what about sounds? What can you hear?
JOHN: I dunno. Um ... Maybe a magpie?
No. A kookaburra. Yeah. There's a kookaburra laughing. And ... it's dumb, but I think for a second—the hills are laughing at me.
Dumb.
THERAPIST: Where are your brothers?
JOHN: They've run off ahead.
THERAPIST: Do you chase after them?
JOHN: Yeah, but I can't keep up. I have to stop to catch my breath. My arm's ... That's right. My left arm's in a cast. It's broken. Healing. My whole side aches.
I ... I fell off the trampoline a week before. Peter and Michael were kicking a ball to each other. Michael kicked it right into my face. I slipped. Fell from the trampoline. Landed on the bricks.
So much pain.
THERAPIST: Bring it back to that day.
JOHN: Um, yeah, so, um, there's this pain in my side. Arm in a cast. Peter and Michael running ahead.

Mum's calling out to us. To wait for her. She's lagging behind, slowly making her way up the trail. I don't want her to catch up to me so … I just run.
I try to run fast, to catch up, reach them, but it's hard with my cast, to get momentum.
I almost slip, have to grab the rock face with my free hand.
I can hear them at the top. Yelling.
I speed up, push through the pain in my side, try to reach them.
But when I get to the top …
I get to the top.
And Peter's on his knees. Crying.
And Michael's gone.

THERAPIST: Yelling?

JOHN: What?

THERAPIST: You said … you said they were yelling?

JOHN: Um … yeah. They were … um …
I'm running, trying, trying to reach them, aching, and they're, um, yelling. Yeah.

THERAPIST: What are they yelling?

JOHN: I dunno … I … I can't …
I can hear the noise but the words are …
It's … it's angry.

THERAPIST: How do you mean?

JOHN: They're angry. They're both so angry.

THERAPIST: At who?

JOHN: I don't know, I don't know, I don't …
I can hear them yelling, my side aches, I'm gasping for breath, I'm trying to run, trying to reach them, but …
I get to the top of the hill, and the yelling grows louder, but there's only Peter, on his knees. And …

Pause.

THERAPIST: What is it?

JOHN:	No, that's not … That can't be … Fuck, no, / that's not …
THERAPIST:	What? What is it?
JOHN:	When I get to the top. He's still there. Michael. They're both still there.

SCENE THREE

PETER:	Thanks for letting me crash.
JOHN:	It's your house too.
PETER:	Ha! It's really not. God, it's like being seventeen. I should go vomit in the pot plants. 'Vomit? No, no, no, that's fertiliser.' Sorry, sorry, we should whisper, Mum might hear.
JOHN:	She's away.
PETER:	I know, I know, I was joking, it's a joke.

Pause.

Tonight was fun. A bit tame.
What did we do for your bucks? Didn't, um, didn't we take you skinny dipping, steal your clothes and leave you at the beach?

JOHN:	Yeah.
PETER:	That was a fun night.
JOHN:	I'll get you a towel.

JOHN *goes to leave.*

PETER: Hey, hey. Don't go. Stay. Chat. We've barely spoken all night.

JOHN *stays.*

Silence.

Are you good?

Pause.

JOHN: Yeah.

Silence.

PETER: How is Mum?
JOHN: What do you mean?
PETER: How is she?
JOHN: When did you last speak to her?
PETER: I can't remember.
JOHN: She's fine.
PETER: Keeping busy?
JOHN: She's painting again.

Pause.

She used to paint when she was younger.

PETER: Yeah, yeah.
JOHN: She wanted to be an artist.
PETER: Yeah, I know, I know.
Are you okay?
JOHN: I'm fine.
PETER: You don't seem /
JOHN: I …
Mum's been working on this one tiny canvas for weeks. Reproducing a photo from my eighteenth. You, me and her, smiling for the camera.
But in the painting, she's … she's painted Michael. All grown up. Standing there with us.

Pause.

I've been seeing a therapist.
It was just … just a custody, court order thing. Just tick a box, mentally sound. Tick.

Pause.

We never talk about him.

PETER: I don't want to.

JOHN:	I think we should. I think it's healthy that we air our grievances.
PETER:	Grievances? What are you—grievances?
JOHN:	It's important for me and it's important / for our relationship.
PETER:	Why, why, why do we need to?
JOHN:	There are unresolved issues that need to be / addressed.
PETER:	Why are you talking like / that?
JOHN:	We need to get closure on this so would you please just / open up to me?
PETER:	Can you just talk to me like a / human being?
JOHN:	How did Michael die?

Silence.

PETER:	What?
JOHN:	Can you just— Would you please answer the question?
PETER:	You know how he died.
JOHN:	Say it.
PETER:	We were hiking. He fell.
JOHN:	No. No, he didn't. That's never made sense. Never made any sense. How do you just fall? How does someone just fall? But that's what you said happened. And why would you lie?

Pause.

    I remember. I remember what happened.

PETER:	What are you talking about?
JOHN:	I remember.
PETER:	You weren't there.
JOHN:	Yes, I was.
PETER:	We left you behind. / You couldn't keep up.
JOHN:	No. I was there. I saw. He didn't fall.
PETER:	He— Yes he did, he / fell.

JOHN:	No. He didn't. I saw.
PETER:	What? What do you think you saw?
JOHN:	I saw what happened.
PETER:	You know what happened.
JOHN:	He didn't fall.
PETER:	It was an / accident.
JOHN:	Just say it.
PETER:	Just a stupid / accident.
JOHN:	He didn't fall. / Did he?
PETER:	Just a …
JOHN:	Did he?
PETER:	Just a … / stupid …
JOHN:	Did he?
PETER:	Just …
JOHN:	Say it!
PETER:	No.
JOHN:	No?
PETER:	He didn't fall.

Silence.

JOHN:	Fuck. Oh … fuck. How could you …?
PETER:	Don't.
JOHN:	How can you even …?
PETER:	Please.
JOHN:	I … why, why would / you
PETER:	I'm sorry, I'm sorry.
JOHN:	Sorry? Don't … don't even … Fuck.
PETER:	I sorry, I'm so sorry.
JOHN:	Don't …
PETER:	It's all my fault, it's all / my fault.
JOHN:	How could—how could / you—?

PETER:	I didn't think he'd do it. I really didn't think / he'd do it.
JOHN:	What? Do what? Fall? Die?
PETER:	I, I didn't, I just didn't think he'd / do it.
JOHN:	So you pushed him?
PETER:	What? I didn't … I didn't push him. I didn't push him. He jumped.

SCENE FOUR

PETER:	We're in the car. You wedged in between me and Michael. Mum singing along to the radio. We're playing 'I Spy'. You keep choosing / trees.
JOHN:	Trees.
PETER:	Michael's rolled up the ten dollars I paid him. I lost a bet over whether you'd jump off the … He's rolled it up and he's smoking it like a thin blue cigarette. He leans over you. Taps invisible ash onto my leg. His arm bumps your sling.
JOHN:	Cast.
PETER:	What?
JOHN:	Cast. I broke it.
PETER:	You strained it. It was in a sling.
JOHN:	No, I … I had an x-ray.
PETER:	Yeah, and it was fine.
JOHN:	I … I don't have your name on my arm?
PETER:	No. Michael leans against your sling. And you …

Pause.

JOHN: I whimper.
PETER: Yeah. Then you ask for a puff.
JOHN: He hands it to me.
PETER: He goes to hand it to you. But he hesitates. Looks over at me. Like I might have recruited you to get it back.
He doesn't hand it to you.
He presses it against the back of the seat in front of him. Flattens it out. Shoves it back into his pocket.
There's a dark rectangle left in the furry seat cover. He rubs his hand along it. Wipes the shape away.
JOHN: Smoking gives you cancer anyway.
Never say yes to a cigarette.
PETER: We pull up at the carpark. Half full.
Me and Michael run ahead. Start on the steepest trail. So you and Mum don't have a chance to say no.
JOHN: Wait up.
PETER: We've left you behind. We're halfway up the hill.
Magpies warbling.
JOHN: Kookaburras laughing.
PETER: Kookaburras laughing. Magpies warbling.
We're halfway up the hill. We've left you behind.
And I say to Michael, 'How about double or nothing? Race you to the top.'
Michael's hand strays to his pocket.
He doesn't say yes or no. Just breaks out into a run.
Bastard.
I'm off.
JOHN: Come back. Come back. Wait for me.

Silence.

PETER: Come with us.
JOHN: What?
PETER: Race with us.
JOHN: That didn't happen.
PETER: Do you want to see what happened?

JOHN:	I fell off the trampoline. I'm still sore.
PETER:	You're feeling better now.
JOHN:	I don't know.
PETER:	Come. Race with us. It's me, Michael and you.

Silence.

JOHN:	I'm running faster than I ever have before.
PETER:	You're almost as fast as me.
JOHN:	I'm gaining on you.
PETER:	We're neck, neck and neck.
JOHN:	We get to the top.
PETER:	I get there first.
JOHN:	You win the race.
PETER:	The debt's cleared.

Pause.

JOHN:	Let's go home now.
PETER:	John.
JOHN:	The debt's cleared. Let's go home.
PETER:	Michael. I bet you can't jump to the other side of the cliff.
JOHN:	No.
PETER:	Just from this ledge to the next. Just over that gap.
JOHN:	Stop.
PETER:	If you really wanna keep that ten. But if you're too much of a pussy …
JOHN:	Is this why he hits you?
PETER:	What? He doesn't hit me. He's bragging about long jump. How that gap's nothing. He can clear that easy.

JOHN:	He can't.
PETER:	I don't think he'll actually jump.
JOHN:	He will.
PETER:	He starts to stretch. Balancing on one leg. Hand round his ankle.
JOHN:	Peter, let's go home.
PETER:	Moves to take a run-up.
JOHN:	Michael, let's go home.
PETER:	Starts to run.
JOHN:	Stop.
PETER:	Full pelt.
JOHN:	Stop him. Stop / him.
PETER:	Straight at the cliff.
JOHN:	Stop!

JOHN *throws himself between the envisioned figure of* MICHAEL *and the edge of the cliff.*

PETER: John!

JOHN *is knocked to the ground.*

Silence.

JOHN: I ... I jumped in front of him.

Silence.

I jumped in front of him ... and we both fell over. Onto the ground.

PETER: You ...

JOHN: And he calls me a dick. For getting in his way. He storms off.
I've rolled my ankle.

PETER: I don't ... know if ... I ...

JOHN: But we're okay. We're both okay. You help me up.

Silence.

Slowly, PETER *moves to* JOHN *and helps him up from the ground.*

	And then we go home. No crying. No screaming. No weird looks at school. No counsellors. We go home. And that night …
PETER:	We play Monopoly.
JOHN:	It goes for eight hours.
PETER:	I'm the iron.
JOHN:	I'm the dog. / Michael's the car.
PETER:	Michael's the car. I loan Michael enough money to build hotels on Mayfair and Park Lane.
JOHN:	He sends me bankrupt.
PETER:	Yeah.
JOHN:	Yeah.

Silence.

MICHAEL: You never went bankrupt.

Pause.

JOHN: / Michael?
PETER: Michael?

SCENE FIVE

MICHAEL *is lying on the sofa, asleep.*
PETER *and* JOHN *watch him.*

PETER:	I thought … I don't know.
JOHN:	We'd made him up?
PETER:	Yeah. What are we gonna do with him?
JOHN:	He can stay here.
PETER:	And what about when Mum gets home?
JOHN:	You don't think she's gonna be happy to see him?
PETER:	How do we explain who he is?
JOHN:	She'll take one look at him and she'll know.
PETER:	And then she'll die of a heart attack and then we'll have even more to explain.

JOHN: Not to her at least.
PETER: That's true.

They watch MICHAEL *sleep.*

JOHN: God, he got old.
He looks so peaceful.
Michael.

Pause.

Michael.

PETER *leans over and pokes* MICHAEL.

MICHAEL *sits bolt upright.*

MICHAEL: What … time is it?
PETER: Ten past nine.
MICHAEL: Why am I … awake?
JOHN: Peter poked you.
PETER: You were saying his name.
JOHN: I wasn't trying to wake him.
PETER: Yes you were.
JOHN: How do you know what / I was doing?

MICHAEL *raises his hand, moves it to his mouth, and presses his index finger to his lips.*

MICHAEL: Shhh. It feels like a woodpecker crawled inside my ear, laid eggs in my brain and now they've all hatched at once and set to work.

PETER *and* JOHN *speak in whispers.*

PETER: Sorry.
JOHN: Sorry.
PETER: We were thinking about making breakfast.
JOHN: Do you still like pancakes?
PETER: We thought we might make pancakes.
MICHAEL: Might … make … pancakes?
PETER: Yeah.

JOHN:	Is that okay?
MICHAEL:	I'm going to sleep now. Wake me up with, 'What would you like on your pancakes?' Actually, after that. Lemon and sugar.
JOHN:	We don't /

MICHAEL groans.

We don't have any lemons.

Pause.

PETER:	Do you wanna—you know—start?
JOHN:	I don't mind if you want to.
PETER:	I'm not really good at pancakes.
JOHN:	They're pretty simple.
PETER:	See, you got this. Thanks, John.
JOHN:	Oh. Okay.

JOHN moves away from MICHAEL.

PETER watches his brother sleep.

A mobile phone starts to ring.

MICHAEL groans.

PETER: John.

MICHAEL groans.

The phone keeps ringing.

John!

MICHAEL groans louder.

JOHN re-enters.

The phone stops ringing.

JOHN:	What?

PETER hands the phone to JOHN.

PETER:	Ah, there was a call for you.
JOHN:	Not mine.

PETER: Then …

               MICHAEL *groans, and shifts to sit upright.*

               He rubs his face. Opens his eyes.

MICHAEL: Who was it?
PETER: Ah … Aaron?
MICHAEL: I never should've told him I was coming back. Now he'll want to catch up. Why did you let me text last night?
JOHN: You told other people you were coming back?
MICHAEL: I hope it's just him. Let me look.
PETER: Who's Aaron?
MICHAEL: Aaron.
               Aaron Aaron.

               Beat.

               My ex-boyfriend.

               Beat.

PETER: Oh.
JOHN: Ah.
PETER: Right.
JOHN: Aaron.
PETER: Good.

               He squeezes MICHAEL*'s shoulder.*

               Good, good, good.
MICHAEL: That … kinda hurts.
PETER: Sorry.
JOHN: Aaron.
PETER: Sorry about that.
MICHAEL: What is with your nails?
PETER: Sorry.
MICHAEL: I need food. What's happening with / breakfast?
JOHN: Oh, I was just about to start.
MICHAEL: Thanks, John. You're the best.

PETER: No, no, I'll do it.
JOHN: What?
PETER: I'll cook.
JOHN: You don't know how.
PETER: It's pancakes, not rocket science.
JOHN: That's not a food.
MICHAEL: Would someone just cook?
PETER: I've got it.
MICHAEL: Thank you.
JOHN: But /
PETER: You can stay here with Michael.
JOHN: Okay.

PETER squeezes MICHAEL's shoulder.

PETER: Good. Good, good, good.

PETER exits.

Silence.

JOHN: We should do something today.
 The three of us.
MICHAEL: So long as it doesn't involve, you know, moving. Noise.
JOHN: I was thinking the beach?
MICHAEL: Sand, salt water.
JOHN: The zoo?
MICHAEL: Animals.
JOHN: Go-karts.
MICHAEL: Moving ... noise machines.

Pause.

JOHN: There's this new cafe down the road.

Pause.

MICHAEL: Go on.
JOHN: We could go there after pancakes.
 They do amazing milkshakes.

MICHAEL: I'm lactose intolerant.
JOHN: Oh. Well, you can have a juice. They make good juice. The pineapple and guava juice / is
MICHAEL: Pineapple is the worst thing for my mouth ulcers.
JOHN: Oh, sorry, / I
MICHAEL: It's fine.
JOHN: Maybe I'll just take you there and you can look at the menu.
MICHAEL: Yeah.
I'm leaving tonight, though.
JOHN: Leaving?
MICHAEL: Yeah, my flight's at six.
JOHN: Where are you … where are you going?
MICHAEL: Home.

Beat.

JOHN: What's it like?
MICHAEL: What do you mean?
JOHN: Your … your home, what's it like?
MICHAEL: It's fine. The roof leaks.
JOHN: Ha! I've never thought of it like that.
MICHAEL: You know the offer still stands.
JOHN: Offer?
MICHAEL: You should come stay with us.
It's not exactly the Hilton, but we've got a futon. It's pretty comfortable. I've slept on it a few times.
JOHN: Us?
MICHAEL: Yeah. He really misses you.
JOHN: Does He?
MICHAEL: Never shuts up about it. Sometimes I think he likes you more than me.
JOHN: Oh, I'm sure He loves us both the same.
MICHAEL: I know, I think so too.
JOHN: He loves everyone the same.

MICHAEL: He doesn't really like Peter.
JOHN: Well …

Beat.

I would love to visit your home.
MICHAEL: Great. That's really— Oh, I can't wait to tell Blair. He'll be so happy.
JOHN: Blair?
MICHAEL: Yeah. He's been a bit lonely. It's just really hard making friends.
The people he works with are all kind of settled. It's just a job for them, you know?
I really was lucky with mine.
JOHN: With your … job?
MICHAEL: Yeah.
JOHN: And … how is it … going?
Your job?
Which you work at?
MICHAEL: Oh, you know.
JOHN: Do I?
MICHAEL: It's fine.
What was the last update I gave you?
JOHN: You …
MICHAEL: Did I tell you about Sarah?
JOHN: Maybe?
MICHAEL: What did I say?
JOHN: Just that Sarah was … up to her old tricks …
Tricksy, tricksy …
How about you just start and I'll jump in if I've heard it already?
MICHAEL: Alright, so you know how they'd been dropping hints?
JOHN: All over the place.
MICHAEL: It was getting a bit awkward, really, because Rashmika came up to me, just the other day, right in front of Paul,

	and said, 'So, I hear you're joining our ranks soon'. I hadn't said anything to Paul!
JOHN:	No!
MICHAEL:	Well, I didn't know it was actually happening yet. No-one had said anything official.

JOHN *shakes his head.*

	So I just freaked out and said, 'Um … maybe. I don't know.'
JOHN:	What else could you say?
MICHAEL:	Exactly. So Paul's staring at me like I'm up to something, Rashmika like I'm an idiot, and I'm mentally willing them both to walk away and not say another word.
JOHN:	And did the … the … the, the … the …?
MICHAEL:	Well, Rashmika—not getting why I'm acting strange, thinking I'm backing out of it—gets a bit aggressive, says, 'Sarah's already started training you. She leaves in a couple of weeks.'
	And Paul's like, 'What's this?'
JOHN:	He's not.
MICHAEL:	Yeah. And then I—I'm not proud of this—I picked my phone up and said, 'How can I help you?'
JOHN:	What's wrong with that?
MICHAEL:	It didn't ring.
JOHN:	Do you think they noticed?
MICHAEL:	I think so.
JOHN:	Wow.
MICHAEL:	Yeah.
	But somehow, fucking miracle, it's all sorted.
	Signed and everything. I start next week.
JOHN:	Congratulations?
MICHAEL:	Thank you. I feel really good about it.
	How are things with you? You still stressed out?

JOHN: Slightly. I would say I'm slightly stressed out.
But, also … good.
Right now I'm kinda good.
It's really good to see you.

MICHAEL: I know. It's been too long.

PETER re-enters.

PETER: How do you flip them without losing the shape?

JOHN: You just have to make sure / the spatula

PETER: Good man.

JOHN: Oh. Yep.

JOHN smiles at MICHAEL. He exits.

PETER looks at MICHAEL. Looks away. Looks back. Looks away.

Silence.

MICHAEL: Are you okay?

PETER: Yep.

MICHAEL: Thought you'd be as bad as me, the way you were going last night.

PETER stares at MICHAEL. Rips his gaze away.

PETER: It was the glass sizes. Deceptive.

MICHAEL: Ah, see I thought it was all the alcohol.

Pause.

PETER: That too.

Pause.

PETER takes hold of MICHAEL's shoulders.

MICHAEL: Hello?

PETER: I'm just gonna say this.
I'm just gonna say this once and then it's out there, it's off my chest and I can breathe.
I can breathe without it crushing me.

MICHAEL: Ah … okay?
Shoot.

PETER: I'm sorry.
I'm sorry I wasn't there for you. I'm sorry I didn't help you. I'm sorry I didn't stop you.
I'm sorry.

Pause.

Wow.
Wow, I actually—
Wow.
I can—
Wow.
I can actually—
My lungs are huge. They are—wow—enormous.
Can you feel that?
This room is so filled with air.

MICHAEL: Right.
What are you sorry for?

PETER: It's fine, I just needed to say it.
You are a beautiful man.

MICHAEL: Thank you.

PETER *hugs* MICHAEL. *Tight. Tighter.*

Th … thank you?

PETER *eventually lets go.*

He smiles.

His smile vanishes.

PETER: Sorry, beautiful was a poor—I didn't mean that in any sort of—you're an adult—grown man—who looks like a—brotherly—natural, perfectly natural—not that there's anything unnatural about—even in nature you'll find—oh, God, what am I trying to—?
Radiant.

MICHAEL: Okay?

PETER: You are a radiant man.

MICHAEL: Thank you. Again.

PETER*'s smile returns.*

PETER: We should all go on a trip.
Camping. We should all go camping.

Beat.

Sorry, that's not offensive, is it?

MICHAEL: You know, for someone who only wanted to say it once, you say sorry quite a lot.

PETER: Sorry. Shit. Sorry. Shit. Sorry.

MICHAEL: You're welcome.

Pause.

There we go.
But, no I hate camping. There's all those … tents and … campfires and—just, no.

PETER: Anything you want. We'll do anything you want.

JOHN *re-enters.*

JOHN: Who's hungry?

PETER: We should take a trip. Don't you think we should all take a trip?

JOHN: I was just saying that we should do something together. Wasn't I just saying that?

MICHAEL: Yes.

PETER: We don't have to camp. We can stay in hotels. My shout.

MICHAEL: Short trip, then?

JOHN: Let's do it.

PETER: Tonight. We should head off tonight.

MICHAEL: I'm leaving tonight.

PETER: What?

MICHAEL: I fly out at six.

PETER: No.

MICHAEL: What's wrong?

JOHN: He has to go home.
But we can visit him.

PETER: You can't leave.

MICHAEL: I'll be back soon.
JOHN: You will?
MICHAEL: The wedding.
PETER: You'll be back for the wedding?
MICHAEL: Well, I was planning to.
I am the best man.
PETER: Of course you are.
Who else would I …?
Of course you are.

PETER breaks down.

MICHAEL: Hey.
Shit, sorry, I, um …

He reaches out and embraces PETER.

There. There.
It's alright.
PETER: Don't go. Please don't go.
MICHAEL: It's okay. It's okay.
Hey, hey, hey.
You're alright. I'm here.

JOHN watches them, then walks towards the door.

Where are you going?
JOHN: I wanna get … lemons.

JOHN hesitates.

He leaves.

MICHAEL: I'm here.
Okay?
I'm here.
I'm right here.

SCENE SIX

PETER *is lying on the sofa, asleep.*
JOHN *enters.*

PETER *wakes with a start.*
JOHN *stands, silent.*

PETER: What's the time?

JOHN *doesn't respond.*

What?
What's wrong?

Silence.

JOHN: I went to get Jessie.
PETER: Where is she?
JOHN: I never told her about Michael.
Not … really.
But all the stories we made up had Princess Jesikah and Prince Michael.
She was gonna meet him. Prince Michael. In the flesh. The flesh …
PETER: John.
JOHN: I drove home. Bek's home.
And I … I …
There was this little old lady. Answered the door.
Hunched. Stank.
I asked for Bek and she …
'Who?'
Bek. Rebecca. Taylor. Bek.
'Who?'
I drove. Left my phone here, so I just … drove. Didn't know where I was going. Passed shops I knew. Houses I knew. Nothing's changed. How can nothing have changed?
And then I … somehow I'm … outside Bek's old house. Where she lived with her ex. Tom.
I'm ringing the doorbell.
The door opens.
It's him. Tom.
Doesn't … punch me in the face. Doesn't … recognise me.

>   Just stares at me. Blank.
>   I go to say sorry, wrong number. But there's a voice from the other room.
>   'Who is it, Tommy?'
>   Bek.
>   I call out, 'Bek! It's John. Can we talk?'
>   She comes to the door and ... her face ... is blank.
>   She says, 'Hello?' like I'm no-one, some ... door-to-door salesman. 'Hello?'
>   And I'm just ... standing there, so, so she goes to shut the door but I yell out, 'Jessie! Jesikah!'
>   They look frightened. Of me. Frozen. Mouths open.
>   And then I hear footsteps. Soft thuds against the floorboards. And there's ... a girl. Five. Six. Jessie's hair. Jessie's nose.
>   Tom's eyes.
>   Tom's lips. Tom's chin.
>   'Who's that, Mum?'
>   Bek doesn't turn from me. 'Go upstairs, Jessie. Go to your room. And shut the door.'
>   I turn. Just ... walk away. I just walk away.

Silence.

PETER *pulls his phone from his pocket.*

He makes a call.

PETER: Charlotte.
Fuck, oh, fuck. Thank you, thank you, thank—
It's ... it's me.
Peter.

Pause.

> You ...

Silence.

> Sorry, wrong ... Sorry.

He hangs up.

Silence.

JOHN:	Did we do this?
PETER:	I …
JOHN:	What have we done?
PETER:	I need to …
JOHN:	Peter.
PETER:	Just, give—just, give me a …
JOHN:	If we did this … If we did / this …
PETER:	I need to …
JOHN:	We can … We can …
PETER:	She didn't … know me. She didn't …
JOHN:	Peter.
PETER:	I just … I just need to just …
JOHN:	Let's go back.
PETER:	What?
JOHN:	To the hike. Let's go back and … Let him jump. We can both just watch. Watch him jump. Fall. Everything can go back to normal. Jessie. Charlotte. Everything.
PETER:	I don't … I don't, I don't know, I don't /
JOHN:	Please.
PETER:	I don't know if I can.
JOHN:	No.
PETER:	I just don't know / if I can.
JOHN:	No, no, no. We're in the car. Mum's singing along to the radio.
PETER:	Hang on, hang on, / I just need to

JOHN: You and Michael burst out the door.
Run off without me.
PETER: John, just, just stop for / a second.
JOHN: I try to keep up but I'm too / slow. Always too slow.
PETER: I need to—please just stop / talking.
JOHN: My side aches but I / push through it.
PETER: John. Just / give me a
JOHN: I reach the top just / after you.
PETER: Just, can you / just
JOHN: You say to Michael, 'I bet you can't jump that ledge'.
PETER: No.
JOHN: Michael says he can. He can clear that easy.
PETER: Stop.
JOHN: He starts stretching his leg.
PETER: Hand round his ankle.

Beat.

What are you / doing?
JOHN: You cheer him on. 'Go on, you pussy. Jump.'
PETER: Jump! /
John. Stop this.
JOHN: He goes to take a run-up.
PETER: Jump, you pussy! /
Stop it.
JOHN: Starts to run.
PETER: Pussy!
John.
JOHN: Full pelt.
PETER: Go! /
Stop!
JOHN: Straight at the cliff.
PETER: Jump!
JOHN: And we just stand there / watching, as he jumps off the cliff and falls to the ground head, neck-first and

PETER: But
you
jump
in front of him!

Silence.

You jump in front of him … and knock him down.
And we all come home.

Pause.

JOHN: No.

Silence.

They are both suddenly conscious of the fact that MICHAEL *isn't present.*

PETER *exits.*

JOHN *sits.*

Time passes.

PETER *re-enters.*

PETER: He's not here.

Pause.

JOHN: Good.
PETER: What did you do?
JOHN: Good.
PETER: John. / John.
JOHN: Good.
PETER: Fuck. We, have we … / Fuck. Fuck.
JOHN: Good.
PETER: Let's go back.
Again.
Stop it from …
Please.
We can find a way to— We can make it good.
Please. I don't … I don't think I can …
JOHN: Good.

PETER: John. I can't …
I can't carry it.
Not again.
Please.
You can't.
It's all you'll ever see.
It's all you'll ever think.
It'll grip your throat and never let go.
You won't breathe.
You won't sleep.
It's always there.
John.
Please.
Come with me.
We're in the car.
John.
We're in the car.
John.

Silence.

JOHN: It's done.

Silence.

PETER *breaks.*

JOHN *is all but vapour.*

Silence.

MICHAEL *enters.*

MICHAEL: Fine. Sorry. I'm shit.
PETER: Michael?
MICHAEL: I freaked out about the tears.
I'm shit.
But I'm back. It's fine. I'm here.
Hello.

Pause.

'Hi, Michael, thanks for coming back. You're so great.'

PETER: Michael?
MICHAEL: Do you want me to leave?
PETER: No. No, I—

    PETER *hugs* MICHAEL.

MICHAEL: There we go.
You're welcome.

    PETER *pulls away.*

PETER: You're okay?
MICHAEL: Yeah. I'm okay. How are you?
And sorry I bailed. Really shit. Tears and—yeah.
Bit of an anxiety thing, freaked out, but all fine. Here to help.
How are you?
PETER: Yeah. Yeah, I'm, I'm / good.
JOHN: Sorry.
MICHAEL: What?
JOHN: I'm sorry.
I'm so sorry. I'm so sorry. I'm / so sorry.
PETER: John just needs—
I'll get you some water, okay?

    JOHN *nods.*

    PETER *exits.*

MICHAEL: Are you okay?
JOHN: I …

    MICHAEL *puts his arm around* JOHN.

MICHAEL: What's wrong?
I practised this in the cab.
Thought it would be Peter, but it's a transferrable skill.
What's wrong … John? I'm here to help.

    PETER *re-enters, unnoticed.*

    He stands, watching his brothers.

JOHN: I … I wanted you to meet her.
MICHAEL: Who?
JOHN: You two would've been …
I really wanted you to meet her. / I wanted you to …
MICHAEL: Who? Who did you want me to meet?
JOHN: I wan … I wanted you to meet …
Je …
Je …
I … Um … J …
J …

Silence.

I can't remember.
MICHAEL: Who is she?
JOHN: I can't …
J …
I can't …
No.
I … I have her face in my head but it's … it's …
J …
I can't quite…
It's …
Gone.

Silence.

It's gone.
MICHAEL: Probably wasn't important.

SCENE SEVEN

MICHAEL: So … What can I say about John and Ellen? Well, in many ways, Ellen's always been like a sister to me. And John's … always been like a brother.

Ba-boom-chi.

Sorry. I promise to not do that again.

John was the best little brother you could ever wish for. He was really fat as a kid so I could use him as a punching bag without hurting my knuckles.

Ba-boo— Sorry. Almost.

John is ... great. He's kind. He's generous. He's warm. He's really fucking smart. And I'm not just saying that because he's really, really rich and I may need to ask for a loan real soon. Like, right about now? We'll talk, we'll talk.

But honestly, the most incredible thing about John is that he's lucky enough to be with someone who's too good for him. Someone who, just by standing there, makes him look like a cruel, stingy, frigid idiot. A full-length mirror.

No, no. Look ... I know John won't mind me saying this ... he was in a very dark place. For a long time. And we didn't know how to help.

Then he met Ellen.

It was like he'd spent years standing on the edge of a cliff. Looking down. And then she came along, and he looked up. He inched back from the edge. He reached for her hand. And he never let go.

Ellen. Thank you for being there. Thank you for being the smart, generous, kind, warm human that you are. John couldn't ask for a more wonderful partner. And I couldn't ask for a better sister.

So charge your glasses. To Ellen. For being the best thing to happen to our family for a very long time. And to Ellen and John. Because together, they shit all over each other.

Cheers.

SCENE EIGHT

JOHN: When the dress broke I thought we were done for. But, no, proving I was right about her, that I am, yes, the luckiest man on earth, she slips through some safety pins and she's back out there.

PETER: She looks beautiful.

JOHN: Thanks.

PETER: I'm not sure that's really—you're welcome.
And the ceremony was … beautiful. Really— What were the, the flowers Ellen was / holding?

JOHN: Lilies.

PETER: Really? I thought—I don't—something else?

JOHN: No, they were / just

PETER: Lilies. There you go.
And, the, the lace thing she had over her face?

JOHN: The veil?

PETER: Ah—veil. Right. Of course. Idiot.
Have you had a chance to— Shit, sorry. No.

JOHN: What?

PETER: Ah … sorry, I know this isn't—
I don't know if I should—

JOHN: What?

PETER: Um … Okay, I—right—I— Sorry to do this now, I know this isn't the best—really, not the best time to bring this up.

JOHN: Bring what up?

PETER: The …
I was wondering if you'd had a chance to—if you'd thought any more about the loan?

Pause.

I know, I know. You've just paid for all this. I mean, you hired out a zoo.

| | And that ceremony, fuck, I mean, yes, I get how that would make anyone …
Beautiful, really—I mean that—beautiful. |
|---|---|
| JOHN: | You said, yeah. |
| PETER: | So I get how you probably can't even think about it just yet, but I really, I mean I would really appreciate it if you could get back to me soon. Not right now, but as soon as you could.
And I'll pay interest. If you want.
And get it all back to you within six months. Seven, eight tops.
I would ask Mum but living with her is bad enough— If I was in debt to her too, you know what she'd be like.
I hate this, I hate putting you on the spot like this, I just didn't want to hassle you before.
You know, I mean, you know I will get it back to you. |

Pause.

So that's it.
That's what I wanted to … ask.

Pause.

JOHN: You're right.

Beat.

Now's not the best time.

MICHAEL *enters.*

JOHN *applauds.*

Well, hello there, Cicero.

MICHAEL:	Thank you, thank you. Didn't think I'd be so nervous.
JOHN:	Nervous? Please, I can smell nerves and you did not smell nervous.
MICHAEL:	What do nerves smell like?
JOHN:	Cheap perfume and cologne. Interns. The new interns at work smell very nervous.
MICHAEL:	Well, I'm just glad it's over.

JOHN:	It was beautiful. Thank you for everything you said.
MICHAEL:	Hey, I meant it.
PETER:	Well done. Wasn't too shit.
MICHAEL:	Thanks.
JOHN:	It wasn't too shit because it wasn't shit at all.
PETER:	Could've done without the … jokes.
MICHAEL:	Are you kidding? That's the whole point of the speech. The father of the bride does soppy. Best man's meant to be funny.
PETER:	Yeah, see there's where I got confused.
MICHAEL:	Oh, ha ha.
PETER:	See, I get laughs.
MICHAEL:	That was irony. You can't claim ironic laughter.
JOHN:	It was great. The jokes were hilarious. Everyone laughed. I laughed a lot.
PETER:	Yeah, but you have to laugh. You're the butt of the jokes. If you don't laugh, you come across as an inhuman prick. And weddings aren't the time for truth.

JOHN *doesn't laugh.*

See, if I'd said that with a mike in one hand and cue cards in the other, you would've laughed.

JOHN:	I should've made you the best man.
PETER:	Yeah. The buck starts here.

Beat.

JOHN:	What did you just say?
PETER:	I …
JOHN:	Just then, what did you just say?
PETER:	I don't …
MICHAEL:	He just wanted to be sure the best man wouldn't sleep with the maid of honour. Nothing like a cliché to curse a marriage.

Beat.

JOHN:	Don't say curse.
MICHAEL:	You don't invoke a curse by saying the word curse.
JOHN:	Stop saying it.
PETER:	Hey, it's not like he said divorce.
MICHAEL:	Divorce, divorce, / divorce,
JOHN:	Shhh. I will kill both of you.
MICHAEL:	So … how long till I'm Uncle Michael?
JOHN:	No. Not any time soon, no, thank you very much.
MICHAEL:	It's just that me and Blair were talking, and we're thinking you should scrap tradition and have two godfathers. He says he'll reluctantly play godmother if that's all that's on offer.
PETER:	You're both atheists.
MICHAEL:	Is that a problem?
PETER:	Sort of, yeah.
MICHAEL:	Oh … I thought the god was just, you know, in title.
PETER:	No.
MICHAEL:	What do you call non-religious godparents?
PETER:	Parents?
MICHAEL:	That can't be right.
JOHN:	There are no babies, and no plans for babies, so no need for any parents, god or otherwise, thank you. Not sure I'm cut out for it, to be honest. I walked past this woman with her daughter the other day, and this little girl was staring at me, just flat out staring. She grabbed her mum and pointed at me, shouted something like, 'That man, Mum, look, that man'. And you should've seen this woman's face. She looked—I don't know—she looked … frightened. Scooped the girl up, ran to the other side of the street and kept running. Didn't look back.

Pause.

	Is it my face?
MICHAEL:	Yes.
PETER:	It is a very ugly face.
MICHAEL:	We've gotten used to it.
PETER:	We've had the chance to.
MICHAEL:	But with strangers it tends to come as—what?—it comes as a /
PETER:	Shock. It's a shocking face.
MICHAEL:	That is the face that sunk a thousand ships right there.
PETER:	It is a very ugly face.
JOHN:	Thanks.
MICHAEL:	I'm really proud of you.
PETER:	Yeah.
JOHN:	What for?
MICHAEL:	For this whole, you know, marriage thing.
JOHN:	I haven't really done anything.
MICHAEL:	Oh, I dunno. It's one of those things, isn't it? Changes everything.
PETER:	Come on.
MICHAEL:	What?
PETER:	Let's go see the pandas.
MICHAEL:	They'll be asleep.
PETER:	No they won't.
MICHAEL:	Wanna bet?
PETER:	How much?
MICHAEL:	I'm not taking your money.
PETER:	What's wrong with my money?
MICHAEL:	It's an endangered species.
PETER:	Fuck you.
JOHN:	Stop.
	There's an open bar. Just … stay.

>   Just for a bit.
>   Just stay.
>   Here. With me.
>
> *They hover.*
>
> *They stay.*

SCENE NINE

GEORGE: I'm going.

ERIC: Don't. All the others have bailed.

GEORGE: I'm not bailing. Just getting another drink and then maybe having a boogie.

ERIC: No-one's dancing.

GEORGE: If I dance, they will come.

> GEORGE *exits.* ERIC *calls after him.*

ERIC: Can you just—?
Yep.

> ERIC *notices that* WILL *is looking at him.* WILL *nods and looks away.*
>
> *Silence.*

Bride or groom?

WILL: Hmm?

ERIC: You here with the bride or the groom?

WILL: I'm here with my sister.

ERIC: I meant who do you know?

WILL: Oh.

ERIC: How are you connected to this whole / thing?

WILL: Oh, sorry. Idiot.

ERIC: Yeah, well …

WILL: What?

ERIC: Bride or / groom?

WILL: Groom.

ERIC: Ah.

WILL:	My sister's just started working for him. Intern.
ERIC:	And he invited her along?
WILL:	Technically she's here as an usher.
ERIC:	What a bastard.
WILL:	Well, yeah. You?
ERIC:	I hope not.
WILL:	What?
ERIC:	Hope I'm not a bastard.
WILL:	No, I meant bride / or groom?
ERIC:	Wait, so how were you invited?
WILL:	Um …
ERIC:	She snuck you in for the free booze?
WILL:	I'm her lift home. Just thought I'd come a bit early.
ERIC:	Dressed for a wedding?
WILL:	Didn't wanna be conspicuous.
ERIC:	Bride.
WILL:	What?
ERIC:	I knew what you— I'm here for Ellen.
WILL:	Who?
ERIC:	The bride.
WILL:	Oh.
ERIC:	You really should not be drinking that champagne.
WILL:	Sorry.
ERIC:	Ex-boyfriend.
WILL:	No.
ERIC:	Yep. High school sweetheart.
WILL:	Oh, this must be awful.
ERIC:	Ah, you know …
WILL:	This must be the most horrible thing. Like something out of a romantic comedy. One that's ultimately unsatisfying because it ends in the heartbreak of the central character. Played by you.

ERIC:	No, it's /
WILL:	When they said that bit, did you almost, you know, rise up in your chair? 'I object!'
ERIC:	It was an amicable split.
WILL:	Oh, God. I am so sorry.
ERIC:	Amicable means it was fine.
WILL:	Sure.
ERIC:	Okay, yes. For a second, I almost, I almost stood up. Okay? / Yes.
WILL:	Understandably. Oh, how awful. This must've been just the most awful day.
ERIC:	Yeah, it / kinda was.
WILL:	Good bubbly, though. A good glass of bubbly always picks me up whenever I'm low.
ERIC:	It's alright.

Silence.

ERIC *moves over to* WILL.

	Eric.
WILL:	Yeah.
ERIC:	Have we met?
WILL:	I should go.
ERIC:	How do I know you?
WILL:	Sorry, I, um, I should really go find / my sister.
ERIC:	Billy Dyson.

Pause.

WILL:	Will.
ERIC:	You've lost weight.
WILL:	You've …
ERIC:	Gained weight?
WILL:	I didn't say that.
ERIC:	I have.

Silence.

WILL: I should really get / going.
ERIC: I'm sorry.
WILL: What?
ERIC: For what happened that night. I'm sorry.
You don't have to believe me.
I've thought about it a lot.
WILL: Me too.
ERIC: Yeah, I … figured.
WILL: When I got that note …
No, I don't want to do this.
ERIC: No, it's alright, I—really. Please.

Pause.

WILL: Deep down I think I knew. It was a cruel joke. I think I knew. I mean, you couldn't have meant any of those things you said. But I didn't … I'm sorry, I can't /
ERIC: Please.
WILL: I should / really go find
ERIC: It's why she left me.
WILL: What?
ERIC: Ellen.
She heard what I did to you that night. Said she never wanted to speak to me again. Took years before she'd even answer my calls. We've only just started being friends. Still don't think she's forgiven me.
WILL: I should've known. I was … stupid.
ERIC: I don't know why I did it. I just heard what you'd been saying about me and I found it so, I don't know …
I just thought … why not? You know?
WILL: You broke my jaw.
ERIC: Yeah.
Sorry.
About that.

WILL:	I was stupid. I should've— *Dear Billy. I think I'm in love with you.* I mean, hello. Fucking idiot, anyone? Right here.
ERIC:	No, I … Before I threw the first punch. I hesitated.
WILL:	I saw. Your hand was shaking. I thought it was nerves.
ERIC:	Maybe it was. Maybe I was nervous.
WILL:	Because you were about to do … what? Something else?
ERIC:	I don't know.
WILL:	If you were nervous … maybe you were hesitant?
ERIC:	Maybe.
WILL:	Maybe you weren't going to hit me?
ERIC:	I don't know. Maybe. Maybe I was gonna …
WILL:	What?
ERIC:	Do something …
WILL:	Kind?
ERIC:	Maybe. Maybe I was going to tell you, you're okay. Everything's gonna be okay.
	Pause.
WILL:	And maybe your hand slips from a fist.
ERIC:	Flattens out. Slides into yours.
WILL:	They meet.
ERIC:	We shake.
WILL:	I smile.
ERIC:	And we're friends.
WILL:	Best friends.
ERIC:	Just like that.
WILL:	We sit together at lunch.
ERIC:	Ellen too.
WILL:	She loves you more than ever.
ERIC:	Falls so madly in love with me.

WILL:	She's the one to pop the question.
ERIC:	On our gap year.
WILL:	Travelling through Europe.
ERIC:	At the top of the Eiffel Tower.
WILL:	No, in the lift on the way up.
ERIC:	She can't help it. Blurts it out.
WILL:	You say yes.
ERIC:	The elevator roars with congratulations in eight different languages.
WILL:	You need a best man.
ERIC:	I ask you.
WILL:	I say yes.
ERIC:	You give the funniest speech anyone's ever heard.
WILL:	I tell them it's easy to make jokes with a subject like you.
ERIC:	You're the first on the floor for the second dance.
WILL:	I cut in, pull Ellen away and put you to shame with my moves.
ERIC:	I don't mind. It's the happiest day of my life.
WILL:	Mine too.

SCENE TEN

MICHAEL: I shouldn't be giving this speech. We shouldn't be here today. When I sat down to write it, I wasn't sad. I wasn't upset. I was angry. My first draft was just eight pages of 'Fuck you'. But then I thought John would actually find that funny, so I binned it.
And I started writing about how I shouldn't be giving this speech. How we shouldn't be here today. How angry I was.
But as I wrote that, I realised I wasn't angry. I couldn't be. Because, no matter how much of a shit he was, no

matter how much he'd get under your skin, no matter how much you wanted to slap him, you could never stay mad at John.

He'd give you that smile, open his arms for a hug, and it all just melted away.

I'm not angry that you left us, John.

I'm just sad.

SCENE ELEVEN

PETER: You spoke really well.

MICHAEL: Thanks.

PETER: I wouldn't have even known how to … Yeah.
Think I would've just ended up reading five pages of 'Fuck you'.

MICHAEL: It was eight.

PETER: Oh, I / was

MICHAEL: Sorry, I'm …
How was Mum this morning?

PETER: Shit.

MICHAEL: Yeah?

PETER: I tried making her eat something, so she finally stopped crying to yell at me. Then went back to crying.

MICHAEL: If you need somewhere else to stay you can / always

PETER: No. Thank you, but … I need to stick this one out. She's … Yeah. Thank you. But no.

MICHAEL: About the ceremony, / too

PETER: Shit, yes, sorry, I was / meaning to

MICHAEL: No, I was gonna say /

PETER: It's just with everything / that's

MICHAEL: It's covered.

PETER: Michael.

MICHAEL: Don't.

PETER: Thank you.

MICHAEL: It's fine.
PETER: I mean, really we should make John pay.
MICHAEL: What?
PETER: I'm just saying. It's not fair to foot you with the bill. But at least he's consistent.
MICHAEL: I want to pay.
PETER: You shouldn't have to. Like you said, we shouldn't be here.
MICHAEL: That's not what I was saying.
PETER: It's literally what you said.
MICHAEL: Fine.
PETER: He was a dick.
MICHAEL: Right.
PETER: Do you not think so?
MICHAEL: No.
PETER: I thought you were just doing that … say what needs to be said thing.
MICHAEL: No, I was doing that say what I mean thing.
PETER: Oh.
MICHAEL: Yeah.
PETER: I mean, he had his good …
MICHAEL: Don't worry.
PETER: It's just like Europe.
MICHAEL: Don't see the connection.
PETER: Just pissing off without a goodbye, without a note. We're all left thinking he's dead until he pops up six months later needing to be bailed out of a German prison.
MICHAEL: Slight differences.
PETER: Well yeah, if he calls us in six months I'll be a bit freaked out.
MICHAEL: He did say goodbye.
PETER: When?
MICHAEL: Last time I was in town.

PETER: What are you talking about?
MICHAEL: Those drinks. He was saying goodbye.
PETER: That was months ago.
MICHAEL: Yeah.
PETER: He wouldn't have know this was gonna happen months ago.
MICHAEL: I think he did.
PETER: You didn't think to mention it?
MICHAEL: I didn't know at the time.
PETER: Then stop trying to— He was fine then.
MICHAEL: He wasn't.
When has he ever bought the first round?
PETER: That doesn't mean / he
MICHAEL: And toasted anything but cheers?
'To the three of us. Together at last.' What was that?
PETER: We hadn't all been together in ages. So /
MICHAEL: It was goodbye.
PETER: He didn't say goodbye. We weren't a part of this. He wasn't thinking of us. He just fucking left.
MICHAEL: No.

Pause.

We're in the bar.
Hidden in a dingy little alley.
He'd picked it out special.
PETER: It's loud, poky and stinks like a gas leak.
MICHAEL: He leads, walking over to a booth.
PETER: I point out the reserved sign.
MICHAEL: He sits down anyway.
PETER: When it's clearly reserved. 'Cause there's a reserved sign.
MICHAEL: A waiter walks over. Asks if he's John.
PETER: It's reserved for us. He reserved a table in a bar.

MICHAEL:	I go to order us drinks.
PETER:	John stops you.
MICHAEL:	'This one's on me.'
PETER:	Scotch, pale, gin.
MICHAEL:	No hesitation.
PETER:	We wait.
MICHAEL:	He asks how we've been.
PETER:	We chat about nothing.
MICHAEL:	We talk about our lives.
PETER:	The drinks come.
MICHAEL:	We reach for our glasses.
PETER:	Move in to cheers.
MICHAEL:	He stops us.
PETER:	He just speaks. He's talking and he keeps talking.
MICHAEL:	He talks to stop us.
PETER:	We stop.
MICHAEL:	Our glasses hover in the air.
PETER:	I spill a bit. Great.
MICHAEL:	He meets my eyes, then yours.
PETER:	He pauses.
MICHAEL:	He raises his glass.
PETER:	Now he spills a bit.
MICHAEL:	He makes a toast. And in that toast he's /
PETER:	Wanting us to thank him for buying the first round.
MICHAEL:	He's saying goodbye. He's saying sorry. He's saying he loves us.
PETER:	He's …
MICHAEL:	He's saying he'll miss us.
PETER:	He's saying …
MICHAEL:	Forgive me.

Pause.

PETER: His eyes meet yours. Then mine.
MICHAEL: Our glasses hover in the air.
PETER: We know what this means.
MICHAEL: We understand the significance of this moment.
PETER: We let it take as long as it needs.
MICHAEL: Until the glasses start to move.
PETER: Drawn to each other.
MICHAEL: Guiding our hands.
PETER: 'To the three of us.
MICHAEL: Together at last.'

THE END

GRIFFIN THEATRE COMPANY PRESENTS

REPLAY
BY PHILLIP KAVANAGH
2 APRIL - 7 MAY

Replay was co-commisioned by Griffin Theatre Company and Playwriting Australia. The commission was made possible by the generous support of Rhonda McIver.

playwriting
australia

Director Lee Lewis
Designer Tobhiyah Stone Feller
Lighting Designer Benjamin Brockman
Composer & Sound Designer Daryl Wallis
Stage Manager Isabella Kerdijk
With Jack Finsterer, Alfie Gledhill, Anthony Gooley

SBW STABLES THEATRE
2 APRIL - 7 MAY

Production Sponsor

Government Partners

Griffin acknowledges the generosity of the Seaborn, Broughton and Walford Foundation in allowing it the use of the SBW Stables Theatre rent free, less outgoings, since 1986.

PLAYWRIGHT'S NOTE

Memory is the key to who we are. Our identity is shaped by the events of our past – our triumphs and failures, our happiness and sorrow, our pride and regret. But the past is malleable, our memories are constantly reconstructed, and we don't truly remember the major events that shape us, but remember remembering them.

In writing *Replay*, I was driven by the paradox of how our fallible memories can possibly culminate when we are tasked with remembering collectively. How do we form a cohesive record of our shared past? Who holds the power in this remembering? And what happens if we choose to remember things differently?

The family unit is used both as an exploration of how these ideas play out on a personal level, and as an allegory for how larger groups form records of their past. As a nation, say, how we remember our past has profound implications for our present and our future. How is it still our collective choice that January 26 is a day of national celebration? How is our relationship to ongoing wars informed by our annual invocation of the ANZAC spirit? If we can challenge the way we shape these past events, through the manner of their communal remembrance, we might be able to forge very different present identities for ourselves, leading to very different futures.

I'm grateful to all the support I received when I wrote an early version of this work while studying playwriting at NIDA. Particular thanks go to Jane, Sarah, Derek, Peter, Josh, Darcy, Jake, Corey, Finn, Lana, Jules and Tony.

Thank you to Lee for taking a gamble on this shorter work and believing there was something there worth growing. I have been so invigorated by our conversations over the past three years, dreaming about what this play could be. I can't wait to get stuck into rehearsals and, together with the excellent team of artists you've assembled, bring *Replay* to life for the Griffin audience.

Lastly, thanks to my family for providing me with the details of my distant and recent past to alter, misremember and skew in constructing a world for these brothers to inhabit. And most of all, thank you to my own brothers: David, Anthony and Mathew. I hope you remember our shared past as more good than bad, like I do. If not, let's talk. I'm sure we can sort it out.

Phillip Kavanagh
Writer

DIRECTOR'S NOTE

I first saw a fragment of this play when Phil was a student at NIDA. Over the years the play has grown, and so has Phil, and so have I and now finally it has found its way onto the Stables stage. From the beginning I have loved the simplicity of a story about brothers and how difficult that can be over time. I have also loved the mystery of memory he is examining. I have loved the freshness of Phil's writing – he is one of a new generation of Australian writers not striving for a voice but using it.

There is gentleness in this play that does not so much interrogate as examine, that does not expose but reveal. Generationally, Phil has grown up in a world where deconstruction is the norm – it stands to reason that this new age of writers will seek to build as their form of revolution.

In a year of some very big grand complicated, loud plays, *Repluy* offers another voice that is as surprising as it can be subversive. The story is very close to home while making us realise that home is something that we are in a constant process of constructing.

And at a time when we are in a desperate battle to construct a home in this country that is intelligent and inclusive, it is a reminder that our habit of forgetting the past will ultimately undermine our hopes for the future.

Lee Lewis
Director

Phillip Kavanagh
Playwright

Phillip Kavanagh is a playwright based between Adelaide and Sydney. His writing credits include: for the State Theatre Company of South Australia (STCSA)/Brink Productions: an adaptation of Molière's *Tartuffe*; for Tiny Bricks/Brink Productions/Adelaide Festival 2016: *Deluge*; and for STCSA: *Jesikah*. Phillip completed a Bachelor of Creative Arts (Honours) and a Master of Arts in Creative Writing at Flinders University, and a Graduate Diploma of Dramatic Art (Playwriting) at NIDA. Phillip has been awarded the Patrick White Playwrights Award, the Jill Blewett Playwrights Award, the STCSA Flinders University Young Playwrights Award and the Colin Thiele Creative Writing Scholarship.

Lee Lewis
Director

Lee is the Artistic Director of Griffin Theatre Company and one of the Australia's leading directors. Her credits for Griffin include: *A Rabbit for Kim Jong-il, The Bleeding Tree, Masquerade* (co-directed with Sam Strong), *Emerald City, The Serpent's Table* (co-directed with Darren Yap), *The Bull, The Moon and the Coronet of Stars, A Hoax, Silent Disco, The Call, The Nightwatchman*; for Sydney Theatre Company: *Honour, ZEBRA!* and *Love Lies Bleeding*; for Belvoir: *This Heaven* and *That Face*; for Bell Shakespeare: *Twelfth Night* and *The School for Wives*; and for Melbourne Theatre Company: David Williamson's *Rupert*, which toured to Washington DC as part of the World Stages International Arts Festival and to Sydney's Theatre Royal in 2014.

Tobhiyah Stone Feller
Set & Costume Designer

Tobhiyah graduated from NIDA in 2005 and previously attended the College of Fine Arts UNSW, where she studied Sculpture, Performance and Installation. Her previous set and costume design credits include: for Ensemble Theatre: *My Zinc Bed, Blood Bank, Blue/Orange, Clybourne Park*; for Riverside Productions: *Parramatta Girls*; for ATYP: *Bustown, This Territory, Desiree Din and the Red Forest*; for Tamarama Rock Surfers: *Anna Robi and the House of Dogs*; for Siren Theatre Co: *Human Resources*; for Blacktown Performing Arts Centre: *My Name is SUD*; and for Merrigong Theatre Company: *Camarilla*. Tobhiyah is Co-director of the Architecture and Performance Design studio *Stukel Stone*.

Daryl Wallis
Composer & Sound Designer

Daryl is a composer, keyboard musician, vocal coach and musical director. Composition credits include: for Griffin Theatre Company/Riverina Theatre Company: *Wicked Sisters* (national tour); for Belvoir: *The Gates of Egypt*; for Ensemble Theatre: *The Violet Hour, Kimberly Akimbo* and *Frankenstein*, winning the 2013 Sydney Theatre Award for Best Score and Sound Design in a Mainstage Production with Elena Kats-Chernin; for Studio Company/Riverside Theatres: *King Lear*; for Merrigong Theatre Company: *Camarilla*; for Siren Theatre Co: *Wanna Go Home, Baby?, Blue Heart, Connie and Kevin and the Secret Life of Groceries, Frozen* and *Human Resources*; and for the Lifestyle food channel: *Heat In The Kitchen*. Daryl also won first prize in the 2012 Federation Bells Composing Competition. His most recent work in sound design includes: for Griffin Independent/Apocalypse Theatre Company: *The Dapto Chaser*; for CDP: *Mr Stink*; for Monkey Baa Theatre Company: *The Peasant Prince*; and for Merrigong Theatre Company/Circa: *Landscape with Monsters*.

Benjamin Brockman
Lighting Designer

Benjamin's lighting design credits include for Griffin Independent/Stories Like These: *Music*; for MEI Entertainment: *Smurfs Live On Stage* (world tour); for Squabbalogic: *Grey Gardens The Musical, Mystery Musical* and *Man of La Mancha*; for Supply Evolution: *Bring It On The Musical*; for Darlinghurst Theatre Company: *Detroit* and *Tinderbox*; for Redline Productions: *Masterclass*; for Tamarama Rock Surfers: *Animal/People*; for New Theatre: *When the Rain Stops Falling*; for Old 505: *River*; for Outhouse Theatre Company: *The Aliens*; for Mad March Hare Theatre Company: *Dark Vanilla Jungle*; for The Kings Collective: *The Wonderful World of Dissocia*; and for Loudmouth Theatre Company: *Those Who Fall in Love Like Anchors Dropped On the Ocean Floor*. His production design credits include: for Loudmouth Theatre Company: *Those Who Fall in Love Like Anchors Dropped On the Ocean Floor*; and for the Old Fitz: *Wittenberg*.

Isabella Kerdijk
Stage Manager
Isabella graduated from Production at NIDA in 2008. Her stage management credits include: for Griffin Theatre Company: *And No More Shall We Part,* and *This Years' Ashes*; for Griffin Theatre Company/Malthouse Theatre: *Ugly Mugs*; for Belvoir: *Jasper Jones, Mother Courage, Kill The Messenger, The Glass Menagerie, 20 Questions, Stories I Want to Tell You in Person* (national tour), *Thyestes* (European tour); for Darlinghurst Theatre Company: *Ride & Fourplay*; for Ensemble Theatre: *Rain Man* and *The Ruby Sunrise*; for Spiegelworld: *Empire*; for Circus Oz: *Cranked Up*; for Louise Withers and Associates: *The Mousetrap* (Australian/NZ tour); and for Legs On The Wall: *Bubble*. Her production coordinator credits include: for Opera Australia/Handa Opera on Sydney Harbour: *Carmen*; and for A-List Entertainment: *Puppetry of the Penis* (production manager/stage manager). Isabella has also worked on various festivals including Sydney Festival and Woodford Folk Festival.

Jack Finsterer
Michael / Therapist / Fric
Jack's theatre credits include for Griffin Theatre Company: *Don't Say The Words, The Emperor of Sydney* and *The Woman With Dogs Eyes*; for Sydney Theatre Company: *Cyrano de Bergerac, Third World Blues, Titus Andronicus*; for Riverside Theatres: *Shellshock*; and for Perth Theatre Company: *Miss Julie*. Jack's film credits include *Kokoda, Spider Walk, How to Change in 9 Weeks* and *Is This the Real World*. His television work includes *Winter, The Doctor Blake Mysteries, Mr & Mrs Murder, Miss Fisher's Murder Mysteries, City Homicide, Rush, Neighbours, Sea Patrol, Dream Life, Dangerous, McLeod's Daughters, Farscape,* and *Blue Heelers*.

Anthony Gooley
Peter / Will

Anthony's previous stage credits include for Griffin Independent/Cry Havoc: *Orestes 2.0*; for Griffin Independent/Two Birds One Stone: *S-27*; for the State Theatre Company of South Australia: *The Glass Menagerie*; for Sydney Theatre Company: *The Lost Echo*; for Sport For Jove: *Of Mice and Men, The Crucible, A Doll's House, Othello, Twelfth Night, The Comedy Of Errors* and *The Libertine*, for which he won the 2011 Sydney Theatre Award for Best Actor in an Independent Production; for Ensemble Theatre: *Death Of A Salesman*; for Theatre Ink/Riverside Theatres: *Angels In America*; for Darlinghurst Theatre Company: *Good Works, All My Sons*; for Cry Havoc: *Three Sisters, Julius Caesar*; and for Tamarama Rock Surfers: *Empire: Terror On The High Seas* and *Rope*. His television credits include: *Underbelly 3: The Golden Mile, Packed to the Rafters, Tough Nuts, Satisfaction* and *Home and Away*. Anthony also works as a director. Recent credits include for Kings Collective: *Gruesome Playground Injuries*; and for the Old Fitz Theatre: *Orphans*.

Alfie Gledhill
John / George

The urge to hear and share stories has been integral to Alfie since his early childhood. Born in the Solomon Islands to a Kiwi father and Native mother, he has worked across stage, film and television since his Sydney stage debut as Romeo in ATYP's *Cursed Hearts*, an adaptation of Romeo and Juliet. His film credits include *Circle of Lies* and *Dario*, a short film for Boomgate Films and Screen Australia. Alfie's television credits include *Hiding* and *Studio3* for ABC, and *The Gods Of Wheat Street* for ABC and Blackfella Films.

ABOUT GRIFFIN THEATRE COMPANY

For nearly 40 years, Griffin has been dedicated to bringing the best Australian stories to the stage. We have a passion for developing Australian talent, with many of our nation's most celebrated artists starting their professional careers with us.

Griffin is a major force in shaping the future of Australian theatre. It is a home for the courageous and the curious, for the imaginations that inspire us. Iconic Australian stories such as *Lantana*, *The Boys*, *Holding the Man* and *The Heartbreak Kid* had their world premieres at Griffin.

Griffin produces an annual subscription season of four to five Main Season shows by Australian playwrights, and co-presents a season of new work with leading independent artists and special events from producers around the country. We also support artists through professional development opportunities, artist residencies and masterclasses.

Our home is the historic SBW Stables Theatre, Sydney's most intimate and compelling space for writers, actors and audiences to meet. We hope to see you here soon.

GRIFFIN THEATRE COMPANY
13 CRAIGEND ST
KINGS CROSS NSW 2011

02 9332 1052
INFO@GRIFFINTHEATRE.COM.AU
GRIFFINTHEATRE.COM.AU

SBW STABLES THEATRE
10 NIMROD ST
KINGS CROSS NSW 2011

BOOKINGS
GRIFFINTHEATRE.COM.AU
02 9361 3817

STAFF

Patron
Seaborn, Broughton and Walford Foundation

Griffin acknowledges the generosity of the Seaborn, Broughton and Walford Foundation in allowing it the use of the SBW Stables Theatre rent free, less outgoings, since 1986.

Board
Bruce Meagher (Chair), Sophie McCarthy (Deputy Chair), Tim Duggan, Patrick Guerrera, Lee Lewis, Kate Mulvany, Mario Philippou, Sue Procter, Lenore Robertson, Simone Whetton

Artistic Director & CEO
Lee Lewis

Associate Artist
Ben Winspear

General Manager
Karen Rodgers

Associate Producer
Melanie Carolan

Development Manager
Will Harvey

Marketing Manager
Estelle Conley /
Aurora Scott

Publicist
Dino Dimitriadis

Marketing & Administration Coordinator
Lane Pitcher

Production Manager
Damien King

Financial Consultant
Tracey Whitby

Finance Manager
Kylie Richards

Customer Relations Manager
Elliott Wilshier

Front of House Manager
Damien Storer

Front of House & Bar
Renee Heys, Nicola James, Julian Larnach, Kristina Paraschos

Studio Artists
Sofya Gollan, Catherine Fargher & Heather Grace Jones, Sheridan Harbridge, Phil Spencer

Writers Under Commission
Mary Rachel Brown
Declan Greene
Michele Lee
Steve Rodgers

Web Developer
Holly

Brand and Graphic Design
RE:

Cover Photography
Brett Boardman

GRIFFIN DONORS

Income from Griffin activities covers less than 40% of our operating costs – leaving an ever increasing gap for us to fill through government funding, sponsorship and the generosity of our individual supporters. Your support helps us bridge the gap and keep ticket prices affordable and our work at its best. To make a donation and a difference, contact Griffin on 9332 1052 or donate online at griffintheatre.com.au

SEASON DONORS

Studio Program
Gil Appleton
James Emmett & Peter Wilson
Limb Family Foundation
Peter Graves
Sophie McCarthy & Antony Green
Rhonda McIver
Geoff & Wendy Simpson
Danielle Smith

Commission $12,500+
Darin Cooper Foundation
Anthony & Suzanne Maple-Brown

Main Stage Donor $5,000 - $10,000
The Sky Foundation
Peter Graves
Abraham James

Workshop Donor $1,000-$4,999
Anonymous (5)
Dr Gae Anderson
Ellen Borda
Jane Bridge
Alex Byrne & Sue Hearn
Richard Cottrell
Ros & Paul Espie
John & Libby Fairfax
Jono Gavin
Larry & Tina Grumley
Judge Joe Harman
James Hartwright & Kerrin D'Arcy
Libby Higgin
Margaret Johnston
Richard & Elizabeth Longes
Elaine & Bill McLaughlin
Dr Stephen McNamara
Ian Neuss & Penny Young
Martin Portus
Sue Procter
Pip Rath & Wayne Lonergan
Merilyn Sleigh & Raoul de Ferranti
Mike Thompson
Jane Thorn
Adrian Wiggins & Siobhan Toohill
Paul & Jennifer Winch

Reading Donor $500-$999
Anonymous (4)
Melissa Ball
Angela Bowne
Bernard Coles
Bryony & Tim Cox
Fiona Dewar
Max Dingle
Wendy Elder
Jacqueline Hayes
Michael Hobbs
Susan Hyde
C John Keightley
Daniel Knight
John Lam-Po-Tang
Jennifer Ledgar & Bob Lim
Rebecca Macfarling & Paul Warnes
Lisa Manchur
Carina Martin
John McCallum
Anthony Paull
Steve & Belinda Rankine
Alex Oonagh Redmond
Karen Rodgers & Bill Harris
Diana Simmonds
Isla Tooth
Judy & Sam Weiss
Simone Whetton

First Draft Donor $200-$499
Anonymous (4)
Priscilla Adey
Jes Andersen
Wendy Ashton
Robyn Ayres
Pamela Bennett
Julie Bridge
Rob Brookman & Verity Laughton
Wendy Buswell
Bryan Cutler
Eric Dole
Susan Donnelly
Tim Duggan
Michele Dulcken
Elizabeth Evatt
Corinne & Bryan Everts
Michael & Kerrie Eyers
Matt Garrett
Sheba Greenberg
Jennifer Hagan
Ross Handsaker
Elizabeth Hanley
Will Harvey & Ester Harding
John Head
Janet Heffernan
Danielle Hoareau
Mary Holt
Val Jory
Ross Kelly
Carolyn Lowry
Ian & Elizabeth MacDonald
Rob Macfarlan & Nicole Abadee
Stephen Manning
Christopher McCabe
Patrick McIntyre
Duncan McKay
Nicole McKenna Kent
Carrington McPhee
Dr Wendy Michaels
Keith Miller
Sarah Miller
Kate Mulvany
Kerry O'Kane
Annie Page & Colin Fletcher
Mario Philippou
Crispin Rice
Rebecca Rocheford Davies
Ellen & Trevor Rodgers
Julie Rosenberg
Catherine Rothery
Dianne & David Russell
Gemma Rygate
Julianne Schultz
Roger Sewell
Jann Skinner
Geoffrey Starr
Augusta Supple
Sue Thomson
Benson Waghorn
Arisa Yura
William Zappa
Aviva Ziegler

We would also like to thank Peter O'Connell for his expertise, guidance and time.

Current as of 03/02/2016

PRODUCTION DONORS

LADIES DAY 2016

Production Patrons
Robert Dick & Erin Shiel
Reay McGuinness
Richard McHugh & Kate Morgan
Bruce Meagher & Greg Waters
Richard Weinstein & Richard Benedict

Production Partners
Cambridge Events
Michael Hobbs
Steve Riethoff
Annabel Ritchie
Diana Simmonds
Jenny & Peter Solomon

THE BLEEDING TREE 2015

Presenting Partner
Gil Appleton

Production Patrons
Peter Brereton
Robert Dick
Richard McHugh & Kate Morgan
Richard Weinstein

Production Partners
Tina & Maurice Green
Jon & Katie King
Bruce Meagher & Greg Waters
John Mitchell
Rachel Procter
Steve Riethoff
Simone Whetton
Carole & David Yuile

You made this.

Production donors make a direct contribution to the costs of staging an individual play, chosen for its unique voice and the strength, insight and candour it brings to the stage. For more information, please contact our Development Manager on 9332 1052.

GRIFFIN FUND

Griffin Fund Donors
Anonymous (1)
Baly Douglas Foundation
John Bell & Anna Volska
Nathan Bennett & Yael Perry
Michael & Charmaine Bradley
Ange Cecco & Melanie Bienemann
Alison Deans & Kevin Powell
Catherine Dovey & Kim Williams
Lilian & Ken Horler
Peter Ingle Kiong Lee & Richard Funston
Lee Lewis & Brett Boardman
Sophie McCarthy & Antony Green
Bruce Meagher & Greg Waters
Dr David Nguyen
Peter & Dianne O'Connell
Ian Phipps
Ian Robertson
Will Sheehan
Stuart Thomas
Simon Wellington & Sanjeev Kumar
Carole & David Yuile

GRIFFIN SPONSORS

Griffin would like to thank the following:

Government Supporters

Patron

2016 Season Sponsor

Production Sponsors

Foundations and Trusts

   GIRGENSOHN FOUNDATION

Company Lawyers

Associate Sponsor

Company Sponsors

  DESIGNKINGCOMPANY

Griffin Theatre Company is assisted by the Australian Government through the Australia Council, its arts funding and advisory body; and the NSW Government through Arts NSW.

www.currency.com.au

Visit Currency Press' website now to:

- Buy your books online
- Browse through our full list of titles, from plays to screenplays, books on theatre, film and music, and more
- Choose a play for your school or amateur performance group by cast size and gender
- Obtain information about performance rights
- Find out about theatre productions and other performing arts news across Australia
- For students, read our study guides
- For teachers, access syllabus and other relevant information
- Sign up for our email newsletter

The performing arts publisher

www.ingramcontent.com/pod-product-compliance
Lightning Source LLC
Chambersburg PA
CBHW050021090426
42734CB00021B/3370